THE WITHERED ARM

Southern Lines to the Far West

Peter Waller

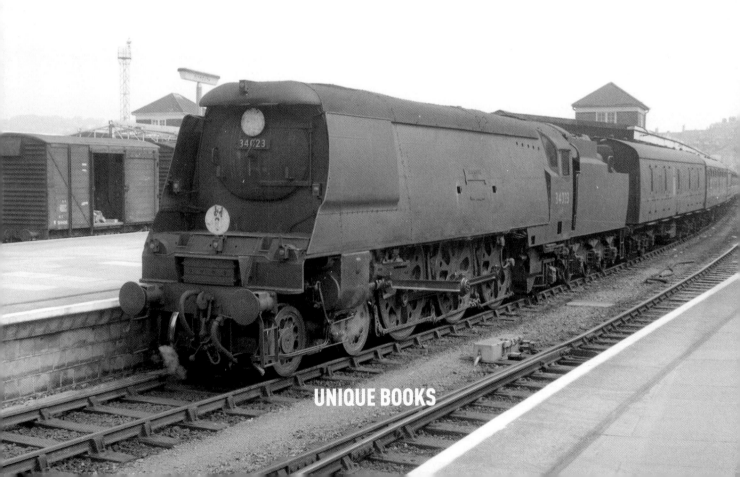

UNIQUE BOOKS

Front cover: All three of the surviving Class 0298 2-4-0Ts – Nos 30586/585/587 – are seen together at Wadebridge on 4 October 1958. *Charles Firminger/Online Transport Archive*

Previous page: Following the closure of the former LSWR station – Plymouth Friary – to passengers in 1958, all services over the Withered Arm to Plymouth operated to or from the former GWR station – North Road (known simply as Plymouth from September 1958) – and it is this station at 11.8am that unrebuilt 'West Country' No 34023 *Blackmore Vale* is pictured on 27 May 1964 awaiting departure with the 11.10am service to Okehampton. *Tony Wickens/Online Transport Archive*

The Withered Arm: Southern Lines to the Far West

First published in the United Kingdom by Unique Books 2021

© Text: Author 2021
© Photographs: As credited

ISBN: 978 1 913555 04 7

A CIP record for this book is available from the British Library

Unique Books is an imprint of Unique Publishing Services Ltd, 3 Merton Court, The Strand, Brighton Marina Village, Brighton BN2 5XY.

www.uniquebooks.pub

Printed in India

A note on the photographs
Many of the illustrations in this book have been drawn from the collection of the Online Transport Archive, a UK-registered charity that was set up to accommodate collections put together by transport enthusiasts who wished to see their precious images secured for the long-term. Further information about the archive can be found at: www.onlinetransportarchive.org or email secretary@onlinetransportarchive.org

INTRODUCTION

The first section of what eventually became the LSWR's network of lines in North Devon and Cornwall to open was the Bodmin & Wadebridge Railway. Authorised on 23 May 1832, the primarily mineral railway opened from Dunmere to Wadebridge on 4 July 1834 with the lines to Wenford Bridge and Bodmin following on 30 September 1834. Although legally not empowered to purchase the line, the LSWR took over in 1847; its purchase was not finally legalised until an Act of 25 June 1886. The line remained isolated until 3 September 1888 when a connection to Boscarne Junction was opened to the GWR's line from Bodmin Road to Bodmin. Prior to this – on 1 November 1886 – the LSWR had suspended its services to permit the line's reconstruction, leaving the GWR to operate the section to Wadebridge alone. LSWR passenger services resumed from Bodmin to Wadebridge on 1 November 1895.

The route from Exeter northwards commenced with the opening of the Exeter & Crediton Railway on 12 May 1851; although backed by the LSWR, this line was built with mixed gauge and initially operated by the broad gauge trains of the Bristol & Exeter until the opening of the LSWR to Exeter on 18 July 1860 and the completion of the link between Queen Street (later Central) and St David's station two years later; standard gauge trains to Crediton commenced operation on 1 February 1862. The LSWR finally bought out the GWR's shares in the Exeter & Crediton in 1879.

The line north from Crediton to Barnstaple (and, in theory, Fremington) was initially promoted by the Taw Valley Extension Railway but this was renamed the North Devon Railway on 24 July 1851. The broad gauge line opened officially on 12 July 1854. For the first year of operation the line was operated by stock hired from the Bristol & Exeter, being replaced then by trains owned by the contractor Thomas Brassey. The next extension – to Bideford – opened courtesy of the broad gauge Bideford Extension Railway on 2 November 1855. Again initially

operated by Brassey, operation of both lines was leased to the LSWR from 1 August 1862. For the first period – until standard gauge track was laid and services introduced (on 2 March 1863) – the LSWR hired Brassey's stock to maintain a service on the broad gauge rails. The line was further extended to Torrington on 18 July 1872.

The line west from Coleford Junction was promoted by the Okehampton Railway (later the Devon & Cornwall Railway). It opened to North Tawton on 1 November 1865, to Okehampton Road (Sampford Courtenay) on 8 January 1867, to Okehampton on 3 October 1871 and to Lidford (Lydford from 1897) on 12 October 1874. Through services were operated to Plymouth over the broad gauge GWR route through the conversion of the latter to mixed gauge.

The LSWR was, however, keen on an independent route to Plymouth and backed the construction of the Plymouth, Devonport & South Western Junction Railway from Lydford to Plymouth and a new terminus at Friary. This line opened on 2 June 1890 and was followed by a branch from Plymouth to Turnchapel opened in 1897. The branch from Bere Alston to Callington followed on 2 March 1908.

The line north from Barnstaple to Ilfracombe was promoted by the LSWR-backed Barnstaple & Ilfracombe Railway, which opened throughout on 4 July 1870. A new station – Barnstaple Town – was provided; this was to become the western terminus of the 1ft 11½in narrow gauge Lynton & Barnstaple line following its opening in May 1898. The L&BR closed, however, on 29 September 1935.

The Bude branch from Okehampton opened as far as Holsworthy on 20 January 1879; it was to be a further 19 years before Bude was connected to the railway system; the extension from Holsworthy opened on 11 August 1898. Prior to this, much of the LSWR's attention had been devoted to the construction of the North Cornwall line from Halwill to Wadebridge and Padstow; this route was opened in stages: from Halwill to Launceston on 21

July 1886, to Tresmeer on 28 July 1892, to Camelford on 14 August 1893, to Delabole on 18 October 1893 and to Wadebridge on 1 June 1895. The final section northwards to Padstow opened on 27 March 1899.

The final link in the creation of the 'Withered Arm' came after World War 1 with the opening of the North Devon & Cornwall Junction Light Railway on 27 July 1925 from Torrington to Halwill. This independent line, engineered by Col Holman F. Stephens, used the trackbed of the earlier narrow gauge Torrington & Marland Railway for its northernmost section. Although operated by the Southern Railway from opening, it remained independent until Nationalisation.

At Nationalisation in 1948, the 'Withered Arm' was initially part of the new Southern Region of British Railways but this arrangement was not to last long as redrawing of the regional boundaries saw the ex-Southern lines running from Cowley Bridge Junction transferred to the Western Region on 1 July 1951. For the travelling public there was probably little indication of the changed control as the locomotives and rolling stock used remained predominantly those inherited from the Southern. Western Region control was not to last long as, on 1 January 1958, the ex-Southern lines were transferred back to the Southern. A final transfer of all the ex-Southern lines west of Salisbury saw the Western Region regain control on 1 January 1963.

By now there were changes to motive power; towards the end of the steam era a number of Ivatt 2-6-2Ts were transferred to the area whilst the three historic Beattie well tanks, which had been a feature of the Wenford Bridge branch for many years, were supplanted by a trio of ex-GWR 0-6-0PTs. More significantly, dieselisation resulted in the appearance of diesel units and locomotives and many of the routes were to see their final passenger services operated by the single diesel railcars produced by either Pressed Steel or the Gloucester Railway Carriage & Wagon Co.

Of the 'Withered Arm' network, as a result of the Beeching Report of March 1963, all of the surviving lines north and west of Exeter – with the exception of the line to Barnstaple and the section from Coleford Junction to Okehampton (which were both to have modified services) – were scheduled for closure. The first section to close was

that from Halwill to Torrington on 13 March 1965; this was followed by Torrington to Barnstaple Junction on 4 October 1965. The next sections to close were those from Bude to Okehampton and from Halwill to Wadebridge, which both succumbed on 3 October 1966 and the section from Gunnislake to Callington on 7 November 1966; the section from Plymouth to Gunnislake via Bere Alston was reprieved, however, although the main line from Bere Alston to Okehampton lost its passenger services on 6 May 1968. Passenger services on the line between Padstow and Bodmin Road and the branch to Bodmin North were withdrawn on 30 January 1967. The final closures were the lines from Barnstaple Junction to Ilfracombe, on 5 October 1970, and from Coleford Junction to Okehampton on 5 June 1972.

Following the withdrawal of passenger services, the sections from Okehampton to Meldon, from Barnstaple to Meeth and from Bodmin Road to Wadebridge along with the branch to Wenford Bridge remained open for freight traffic although, with the exception of the line to Meldon, these routes have now closed completely. The ex-GWR section from Bodmin Road to Boscarne Junction is, however, now preserved and much of the trackbed of the closed routes forms part of a number of popular footpaths and cycleways. There are also plans to see some services restored; whether this will happen, only time will tell.

During September 1963, Class N 2-6-0 No 31842 approaches Bere Alston with an up service from Plymouth. In the background, the line towards Calstock and Callington curves away to the west. Originally designed for the South Eastern & Chatham Railway in 1914 by Richard Maunsell, a total of 80 of this design were built between 1917 – production being delay by World War 1 – and 1934. During the 1920s, in order to relieve unemployment caused by the cessation of hostilities, the government ordered 100 locomotives to Maunsell's design to be constructed at Woolwich Arsenal using boilers supplied by the North British Locomotive Co; of these, the Southern Railway acquired 50 of the kits produced at Woolwich and completed construction at Ashford Works. These locomotives were originally SR Nos A826-75, becoming Nos 31826-75 at Nationalisation. No 31842, one of this batch, was completed at Ashford in August 1924. Based in the West Country for much of its life, the locomotive was allocated to Exmouth Junction when recorded here; it was transferred to Guildford in June 1964 from where it was withdrawn in September the following year.
John McCann/Online Transport Archive

Bere Alston station viewed in the up direction towards Tavistock as a DMU stands in the northernmost platform with a service towards Callington on 17 August 1966. Passenger services on the line between Okehampton and Bere Alston ceased on 6 May 1968; at the same time, the line between Meldon Quarry and Bere Alston closed completely. Since closure, there has been the inevitable rationalisation of track with all services – to Gunnislake and to Plymouth – now all concentrated on the former down platform. Despite this, however, the main station building remains intact whilst the island platform with its shelter and (disused) signalbox as well as the former goods shed visible in the distance are also still extant. There are plans – as a result of a significant housing development at Tavistock – for the reopening of the 5½-mile section east from Bere Alston. The vulnerability of the sea wall at Dawlish – currently the only railway link west of Exeter – has also resulted in renewed interest in reopening the line through to Okehampton.
John Meredith/Online Transport Archive

Callington, where Ivatt-designed 2-6-2T No 41323 is seen awaiting departure with a service towards Bere Alston in September 1963, was the terminus of the of the Plymouth, Devonport & South Western Junction Railway branch and opened – as Callington Road – on 2 March 1908. The route's origins, however, were much older and lay with the 3ft 6in East Cornwall Mineral Railway, which opened officially on 7 May 1872 (although certain sections had been operational before that date). The line was designed to move mineral traffic from mines and quarries in the Callington area to a quayside – accessed by a rope incline – on the River Tamar at Calstock. The ECMR was acquired by the PD&SWJR in 1891 and, linked to the company's route at Bere Alston, was converted to 4ft 8½in. Although operated by the LSWR, the PD&SWJR maintained its notional independence until the Grouping in 1923. Once completed, the branch from Bere Alston was just over nine miles in length. The section from the original station in Gunnislake to Callington, which suffered from road competition and distance from the settlements it purported to serve (Callington station was over a mile from Callington itself), was closed on 7 November 1966.
John McCann/Online Transport Archive

There are less than three months to go for passenger services to Callington when this view of a two-car DMU awaiting departure was taken on 17 August 1966. In the foreground can be seen the small engine shed that served the terminus. Following the conversion of the line to standard gauge in 1894 by the Plymouth, Devonport & South Western Junction Railway, the new operator built a new engine shed to the east of the station; the structure illustrated here, however, had been the result of a rebuild in the mid-1930s when the shed was shortened and was provided with a higher pitched roof. The shed was closed by BR in September 1964 and subsequently demolished.
John Meredith/Online Transport Archive

As the train crew and station staff look on quizzically, the photographer records the token being exchanged at Gunnislake on 17 August 1966. The train, formed of BRCW-built Class 118 DMU Nos W51305 and W51320, was heading to Bere Alston from Callington. Following the closure of the section of line west to Callington in November 1966, Gunnislake was to become the terminus of the shortened branch. Originally an island platform, the facilities were reduced so that only one platform face remained in use. The original station survived until 9 June 1994 when a new station – to the east of the low road bridge – was opened, thus permitting the removal of the bridge.
John Meredith/Online Transport Archive

The Southern station in Tavistock – given the suffix 'North' on 26 September 1949 – was originally opened by the Plymouth, Devonport & South Western Junction Railway on 2 June 1890. Here 'N' class No 31835 is pictured at the station with the Plymouth portion of the down 'Atlantic Coast Express'. This locomotive, built at Ashford Works in July 1924, was to spend the entire period post Nationalisation allocated to Exmouth Junction shed before withdrawal in September 1964. The station – probably designed by Robert Galbraith and Richard Church (the railway's engineers) – was to lose its passenger services with the closure of the section between Bere Alston and Okehampton on 6 May 1968. The station building, which is Grade II listed, still survives and has recently been restored to form holiday cottages. The bulk of the trackbed between Tavistock and Bere Alston remains intact and there are proposals for the restoration of passenger services linked to a new housing development in the town.
W. A. C. Smith/Transport Treasury

The graceful lines of the viaduct at Meldon recorded from the south on 6 September 1953. The 541ft-long viaduct, now a scheduled ancient monument, is one of only two railway viaducts in Britain to survive that were constructed using wrought iron lattice piers to support cast iron trusses. When first opened on 12 October 1874 the viaduct was only single track; when it was doubled in 1874, a second – steel-built – structure was constructed alongside the original and the two bridges were combined.

Following the cessation of all traffic between Meldon and Bere Alston on 6 May 1968, a single track across the viaduct was retained to facilitate shunting operations at the adjacent quarry. However, the deterioration in the condition of the bridge resulted in the final track over it being removed in the early 1990s. Subsequently work has been undertaken on the viaduct and it now forms part of the Granite Way, a 12-mile route linking Okehampton and Lydford. *John Meredith/Online Transport Archive*

Viewed from the train, the quarry at Meldon can be seen to the south of the main line. The first granite to be quarried here for the railways was extracted in 1874 contemporaneously with the opening of the LSWR line from Okehampton to Lydford. However, the major expansion came after 1897; by the early 1950s it was producing some 340,000 tons of granite per annum. It remained railway owned until Privatisation on 4 March 1994. Visible in the shed is No DS234. This 'USA' class 0-6-0T had originally been

No 30062 prior to being transferred to departmental stock in December 1962 when it was transferred to Meldon to replace No DS682 – a Class G6 0-6-0T (ex-No 30238). No DS234 had been officially withdrawn five days before the date of this photograph; the locomotive was cut up at Cashmores of Newport during April the following year. This was the last steam locomotive allocated to Meldon; thereafter Class 08 diesel shunters proved the resident motive power. *John Meredith/Online Transport Archive*

Class T9 4-4-0 No 30709 stands in Okehampton awaiting departure on 3 June 1961 with a service to Bude and Padstow. Designed by Drummond, a total of 66 of the class were constructed at Nine Elms and by the Glasgow-based Dübs & Co between 1899 and 1901 for the LSWR. Nicknamed 'Greyhounds', the locomotives were designed to provide competition to the GWR's express services to the West Country. All were rebuilt by Urie between 1922 and 1929 with superheaters, larger cylinders and higher pressure boilers; this improved further their performance. No 30709 was new in June 1899. By the date the locomotive was recorded here, it was allocated to Exmouth Junction shed and was approaching the end of its operational life; it was withdrawn the following month and scrapped in September 1961.
Marcus Eavis/Online Transport Archive

The new order at Okehampton at 1pm on 27 May 1964 sees 'Hymek' No D7097 about to depart westwards with the 1.1pm service to Plymouth. At this date, the locomotive was relatively new, having been completed by Beyer Peacock in Manchester in December 1963. Based at Cardiff Canton briefly when new, it was transferred to Newton Abbot in late January 1964 and to Laira a month after this view was taken. Like most of the class, No D7097's career was short; withdrawn from Bristol Bath Road in November 1972, the locomotive languished at Swindon until being scrapped in March 1975. *Tony Wickens/Online Transport Archive*

As the footplate crew give the locomotive some minor attention, BR Standard 2-6-4T No 80036 stands in Okehampton station with a westbound service on 27 May 1964. In the background can see seen the goods yard; freight traffic continued to Okehampton until facilities were withdrawn in January 1983. Following the withdrawal of passenger services west of the station on 6 May 1968, the section from Coleford Junction to Okehampton, which had been listed under the Beeching Report of March 1963 to see a modified service, was not to survive long. Passenger services to Okehampton were withdrawn on 5 January 1972 although the line through the station remained open primarily for stone traffic from Meldon Quarry. The station, which remains very much as illustrated here (including the goods shed now converted into youth hostel), has from the late 1990s seen the return of – initially – seasonal summer passenger services and, more recently, the operation of the Dartmoor Railway. The Yeoford-Okehampton section is one of the lines under active consideration as part of the plans to see some of the Beeching era cuts reversed.
Tony Wickens/Online Transport Archive

Pictured on the turntable at Okehampton on 19 July 1949 is 'U' class 2-6-0 No 31628. This class had its origins in Maunsell's 'K' class of 2-6-4Ts, of which 20 were constructed between 1917 and 1925. However, following a derailment at Sevenoaks on 27 August 1927 involving No 800 *River Cray* it was decided to rebuild all 20 as 2-6-0s. A further 30 locomotives – Nos 1610-39 – were constructed to the same design between August 1928 and May 1931. No 31628 was amongst those built in 1929, being completed at Ashford Works during April that year. When recorded here, the locomotive was a relatively recent arrival in the West Country – having been transferred from Reading to Exmouth Junction shed in May 1949 – but its sojourn to the area was short-lived; it was transferred again – this time to Guildford – in February 1950. The shed at Okehampton received a replacement 70ft turntable during 1943; this was situated adjacent to the station and replaced the late 19th century 50ft turntable that had been located in front of the shed itself. The engine shed at Okehampton closed in 1964 and was subsequently demolished.
John Meredith/Online Transport Archive

In September 1963 unrebuilt 'Battle of Britain' No 34083 *605 Squadron* is pictured running round its train at Padstow. This terminus was a relatively late addition to the railway network, the line from Wadebridge not officially opening until 23 March 1899 with timetabled services commencing four days later (although the LSWR had had power to construct the route from Halwill via Wadebridge since 1882). The new station was provided with a single 100-yard long platform with a stone-built building that accommodated the stationmaster's house and offices. In addition,

Padstow also possessed a small goods shed, turntable (increased to 65ft diameter in 1947 to accommodate Bulleid Pacifics) and freight-only branch serving the harbour along with a shed to handle fish traffic. Completed at Brighton Works during October 1948, No 34083 had initially been allocated to Stewarts Lane when new. It was to spend much of its career in Kent – being allocated to Ramsgate, Dover Marine and Ashford – before one final reallocation took it to Exmouth Junction in November 1961.
John McCann/Online Transport Archive

Listed for closure under the Beeching report of March 1963, BR formally applied to close the line from Padstow to Bodmin Road on 21 October 1965 and formal consent was given by Barbara Castle, the then Minister of Transport, on 15 September 1966; passenger services were formally withdrawn over the North Cornwall line on 3 October 1966 and on the route to Bodmin Road on 30 January 1967 (freight facilities had been withdrawn in September 1964). Following removal of the track in 1968, the station building survived and is now used as offices. Pictured in the platform on 17 August 1966 is a southbound diesel railcar; dieselisation of services to Padstow took place in early 1965. *John Meredith/Online Transport Archive*

One of the trio of Beattie well tanks – No 30585 – is seen at the southern end of Wadebridge station in light steam. Joseph Beattie and his son, and successor as LSWR Mechanical Engineer, William designed a number of 2-4-0T locomotives for the LSWR of which the 12 examples of the '0298' class built during 1874 and 1875 were the last. These were constructed by Beyer Peacock in Manchester. Initially designed for use on London suburban services, they were transferred away from 1890 as newer locomotives entered service. Some were rebuilt as tender locomotives but all of the total of 85 2-4-0Ts were soon withdrawn with the exception of six that were rebuilt between 1889 and 1894 for use on West Country branches. Three of these – LSWR Nos 44, 257 and 266 – were withdrawn by 1899, leaving the remaining three operational based at Wadebridge for use on the branch to Wenford Bridge. No 30585 was completed as LSWR No 314 in May 1874; it became LSWR No 0314 on the company's duplicate list in May 1901 and eventually SR No 3314. Withdrawn in December 1962, No 30585 was preserved and is normally based now at the Buckinghamshire Railway Centre.
D. Kelk/Online Transport Archive

The second of the three surviving well tanks – No 30586 – is pictured inside the small shed at Wadebridge. Unlike Nos 30585 and 30587, No 30586 had rectangular rather than round splashers. Completed as LSWR No 329 in November 1875, the locomotive was transferred to the LSWR's duplicate list – as No 0329 – in October 1901 becoming SR No 3329 after the Grouping. Although scheduled for preservation following withdrawal, No 30586 was not as lucky as the other two, being scrapped in March 1964.

The small wooden-built two-track shed at Wadebridge was constructed by the LSWR in 1895 and replaced an earlier structure located further to the north. The shed was extended in 1906 to accommodate steam railmotors (which lasted until 1919) and in 1949 the building was reroofed in corrugated asbestos. Following closure in October 1964, the shed was demolished.
D. Kelk/Online Transport Archive

A hint of the new regime at Wadebridge in September 1959 as ex-GWR '4575' class 2-6-2T 5557 is pictured departing with a service from Wadebridge to Bodmin Road. Completed at Swindon in November 1928, No 5557 was a St Blazey-allocated locomotive when recorded here. By this date it was approaching the end of its 32-year operational career; it was withdrawn in October the following year. *Derek Cross*

With one of the trio of Beattie well tanks shunting in the background, Class O2 No 30199 departs from Wadebridge with a service from Padstow to Bodmin in September 1959. Designed by William Adams, a total of 60 of the 'O2' class were constructed at Nine Elms between 1886 and 1896. Initially, they were designed to operate London suburban services – and thus to supplant the earlier 2-4-0Ts – but were themselves supplanted by more powerful designs from the late 1890s. All of the class passed to the SR in 1923, but a number were withdrawn from the early 1930s whilst others were transferred to the Isle of Wight. In all, 48 passed to BR in 1948. No 30199 was new in June 1891 and when recorded here was allocated to Exmouth Junction; it remained based there until transferred to Eastleigh in November 1961 from where it was withdrawn in December the following year.
Derek Cross

Examples of the two classes of single diesel railcars that dominated services to Padstow and Halwill in the last period of operation can be seen awaiting departure from Wadebridge on 18 August 1966. On the left is Class 121 No W55025 operating a service from Bodmin Road to Padstow whilst on the right Class 122 No W55001 is shortly to head over the line towards Halwill. The station illustrated here was the second to serve the town; it opened as a terminus – courtesy of the LSWR but initially operated over the Bodmin & Wadebridge line by the Great Western – on 3 September 1888. The North Cornwall line from Delabole was opened on 31 May 1895 and the line was extended north to Padstow on 23 March 1899. Passenger services to Halwill were withdrawn on 3 October 1966 and those from Padstow to Bodmin Road on 30 January 1967. It was not, however, until 4 September 1978 that freight traffic over the line south from Wadebridge was finally withdrawn. Today, the main station building, with its canopy, is still extant as the John Betjeman Centre whilst the goods shed also still survives. A housing estate occupies much of the remainder of the station site.

John Meredith/Online Transport Archive

The three well tanks were all withdrawn from service at the end of 1962 and replaced on the Wenford Bridge branch by ex-GWR 0-6-0PTs Nos 1367-69; these were designed with a short wheelbase for use of dock railways – such as the Weymouth Quay line – and so were ideal to replace veteran trio. Here No 1367 is seen shunting at Wadebridge in late 1963. Nos 1366-71 were designed by Charles Collett and were all built at Swindon during February 1934. No 1367 was based at Weymouth Radipole shed until transfer to Wadebridge in August 1962; the trio's career on the Wenford Bridge branch was destined to be relatively short, however, as all three were withdrawn during October and November 1964. Of the ex-GWR locomotives, No 1369 survives in preservation.
John McCann/Online Transport Archive

The survival of the three Beattie well tanks for more than 60 after the withdrawal of the other 2-4-0Ts was due to their suitability for operation over the sharp curves of the freight-only branch to Wenford Bridge. Here the third of the trio – No 30587 – is pictured. New as LSWR 298 in June 1874 – the first of the batch to be completed – it became No 0298 on the duplicate list in June 1898 and SR No 3298 after Grouping. Following withdrawal, No 30587 was preserved as part of the National Collection although it is currently based, appropriately, on the Bodmin & Wenford Railway. *D. Kelk/Online Transport Archive*

The original Bodmin & Wenford station at Bodmin opened on 30 September 1834 when the line was extended from the temporary terminus at Dunmere. The station illustrated here, however, was the result of the modernisation of the line and opened on 1 November 1895. The station gained the suffix 'North' on 26 September 1949 in order to differentiate it from the ex-GWR station in the town, Bodmin General. On 19 June 1962 'N' class 31875 is seen at the station's single platform awaiting departure; this locomotive had been reallocated to Exmouth Junction in February the previous year. Freight facilities at Bodmin North were withdrawn on 24 July 1964 and passenger services ceased on 30 January 1967. Following closure, the station was subsequently demolished and the site is now occupied by a car park. *R. C. Riley/Transport Treasury*

Passengers wait on the platform at Camelford – 'For Boscastle and Tintagel' – for a Halwill-bound service from Wadebridge. This station was unique amongst those on the North Cornwall Railway in possessing a platform canopy – albeit only on the up side (and presumably to offer some protection for travellers heading east who had earlier visited Tintagel Castle, perhaps) – and, like other stations on the line, was some distance – 1½ miles – from the settlement it purported to serve. Bus services linked the station to Camelford itself as well as the popular tourist destinations locally. In 1911 the loop was extended to permit 12-coach trains to pass. The substantial station building is still extant and now provides accommodation for the British Cycling Museum.
Allan Clayton/Online Transport Archive

The patience of the passengers on the up platform has been rewarded as 'N' class 2-6-0 No 31845 awaits departure with a service towards Halwill. Built at Ashford in September 1964, No 31845 was to spend all of its BR career allocated to Exmouth Junction except for three months during June to October 1953 when it was based at Barnstaple Junction. It was to survive exactly 40 years in service, being finally withdrawn in September 1964. *Allan Clayton/Online Transport Archive*

As Class T9 No 30717 awaits departure in the up direction, unrebuilt 'West Country' No 34023 *Blackmore Vale* approaches Otterham station with the down 'Atlantic Coast Express' during September 1959. The crew have the single line token ready to pass over to the signalman. Completed at Brighton in February 1946 as No 21C123, the locomotive was initially allocated to Nine Elms. After a year at Salisbury, No 34023 was reallocated to Exmouth Junction in May 1951. It was to remain a West Country-based locomotive until a move saw it transferred to Eastleigh in September 1964. No 34023 was to haul the last Padstow portion of the down 'ACE' when the service was withdrawn during that month. A final reallocation, in May 1967, saw it return to Nine Elms in May 1967 where it was to be one of the class that survived through to the end of Southern Region steam in July that year. One of only two unrebuilt 'West Country' locomotives in service at that time – the other being No 34102 *Lapford* (which was in a poorer condition) – No 34023 was acquired for preservation. Since 1971 No 34023 has been based on the Bluebell Railway.
Derek Cross

When recorded here, on 18 August 1966, Tresmeer station was approaching closure – passenger services were withdrawn on 3 October 1966 – and already facilities had been reduced. Class 122 No W55001 is seen standing in the down platform with an up service from Wadebridge to Halwill; by this date the up loop was already out of use (the signalbox having been closed on 14 November 1965) and the station had been unstaffed since January 1965. Tresmeer station, which opened on 28 July 1892, was actually situated in Splatt, about a mile north of Tresmeer itself. Apart from the two platform station, there was also a small goods yard – freight facilities had been withdrawn in September 1964 – with agricultural produce, including rabbits, being the major traffic. *John Meredith/Online Transport Archive*

Viewed from a passing down train just before 7pm on 26 May 1964 are the main station buildings at Egloskerry with the signalbox visible in the distant. The station possessed a passing loop with up and down platforms, as a well as a small good yard (although this had closed on 9 May 1960, some four years before the photographer recorded this view). To the west of the station was a level crossing; this was the only one on the section from Wadebridge to Halwill. Following closure on 3 October 1966, the station building was converted into a private house and is still extant. *Tony Wickens/Online Transport Archive*

After Nationalisation, the ex-GWR station in Launceston was closed on 30 June 1952 with all services being concentrated on the adjacent ex-Southern station. On 2 May 1961 ex-GWR 2-6-2T No 5541 is pictured in the up platform. The signalbox on the platform was extended in 1916 when it replaced the Great Western box; the box was widened to accommodate two sets of equipment, one serving each station. Passenger services over the ex-GWR line southwards ceased on 31 December 1962 whilst those on the main line from Wadebridge to Halwill ceased on 3 October 1966. After closure, the railway facilities were demolished and the site is now occupied by an industrial estate although the 1ft 11½in Launceston Steam Railway occupies 2½ miles of the former trackbed slightly to the west of the station illustrated here. The Southern reached Launceston courtesy of the North Cornwall Railway, which opened from Halwill on 21 July 1886. Launceston was destined to be the terminus of the line until 28 July 1892 when the extension to Tresmeer opened. The line westwards was then opened in a number of stages: thence to Camelford on 14 August 1893; to Delabole on 18 October 1893; and, finally, to Wadebridge on 1 June 1895. *R. C. Riley/Transport Treasury*

The penultimate station on the line from Wadebridge to Halwill was Tower Hill and, with two small children clambering on the wire and post fence under the running-in board to watch the passing train, the main station building is pictured from a down train on 26 May 1964. When opened Tower Hill possessed a down loop as well as a signalbox. However, the line through the station was singled from 16 June 1920 and the box abolished, resulting in a seven-mile section from Launceston to Ashwater with a ground frame being installed later to operate the points to the small yard.

However, due to traffic during World War 2, new sidings were installed whilst the down loop and signalbox – the latter being constructed in the former booking hall and extended onto the platforms as shown in this view – were reinstated. The loop and box were taken out of service on 7 November 1965; the simultaneous closure of the box at Ashwater resulted in the section now running from Launceston to Halwill for the last year of the line's operation.
Tony Wickens/Online Transport Archive

Viewed from the buffer stops on 27 May 1964, a two-coach train stands in the platform at Bude whilst a single coach sits at the end of the siding added to the station layout in 1939. Although the LSWR reached Holsworthy on 20 January 1879 it was to be virtually two decades before the 5¾-mile extension opened to the new terminus at Bude on 10 August 1898. The new line was built following a local campaign, backed by the LSWR, for the extension beyond Holsworthy; the Holsworthy & Bude Railway was authorised on 20 August 1883. This, however, failed to be built, being formally abandoned on 20 May 1892, and a further Act – passed on 6 July 1895 – was required before construction started. A short – half-mile – connection ran from the station to the tidal harbour.

Tony Wickens/Online Transport Archive

The 3.11pm service from Bude to Okehampton, formed of 'N' class 2-6-0 No 31856 and two carriages, awaits departure from Bude at 3.5pm on 27 May 1964. Following the closure of the line in October 1966, the stone-built station, which included the stationmaster's house, was demolished and the site redeveloped as a housing estate. Built at Ashford Works in March 1925, No 31856 had been an Exmouth Junction-allocated locomotive at Nationalisation but, between October 1951 and February 1961 (when it returned to Exmouth Junction), the locomotive had been based for periods at Guildford, Hither Green and Redhill. By May 1964 the locomotive was approaching its final few weeks in service; it was stored at the end of the following month and withdrawn in early July.
Tony Wickens/Online Transport Archive

When recorded on 18 August 1966 with single railcars No W55014 and W55026 standing in the platform awaiting departure for Halwill, Bude station was already showing evidence of track rationalisation. With the opening of the line the LSWR provided a small engine shed situated to the south of the station and effectively behind the photographer in this view; the shed, which had provided with a 50ft turntable and coaling stage, had, however, closed almost two years before this view was taken, in September 1964. That month had also witnessed the withdrawal of freight facilities from the station, leaving the line to survive for passenger traffic only until the line to Halwill was closed completely on 3 October 1966.
John Meredith/Online Transport Archive

The main up platform with signalbox at Halwill recorded on 26 May 1964. Originally opened as a station on the Devon & Cornwall Railway on 20 January 1879, it became a junction on 21 July 1886 with the opening of the first part of the North Cornwall Railway – to Launceston – and its importance was to be increased as a result of the opening of the North Devon & Cornwall Junction Light Railway to Torrington on 27 July 1925. The junctions were situated slightly to the north of the station itself. The signalbox illustrated here was opened in 1886 with the Launceston line and extended in 1925 to accommodate traffic to and from Torrington. During World War 2 additional sidings were constructed to the south of the station and an up goods loop installed. The station was known officially as Halwill Junction from 1897 until becoming simply Halwill on 1 January 1923 although one running-in board called the station 'Halwill for Beaworthy'. The station survived (although the signalbox was demolished shortly after final closure), in an increasingly derelict condition, until the late 1980s when it was demolished; a housing estate has subsequently been built on the site.
Tony Wickens/Online Transport Archive

Services to Torrington from Halwill were accommodated at the latter by a short bay platform situated slightly to the north of the main up platform and, on 26 May 1964, Ivatt 2-6-2T No 41214 is pictured awaiting departure with its one-coach train at 6.15pm. The coach is S67643S. Passenger services over the Torrington line ceased on 1 March 1965.
Tony Wickens/Online Transport Archive

On 18 August 1966 Class 122 diesel railcar No W55017 is seen approaching Halwill with a service from Bude. With the closure of the Torrington line the previous year, the bay platform was rendered unemployed and the track has been lifted. Other evidence of rationalisation and modernisation is also apparent; some signalling has been removed and the bag for the water column has also disappeared. The closure has also resulted in the statement on the running-in board – 'Halwill for Beaworthy – Junction for Bude, North Cornwall & Torrington Lines' – no longer being strictly correct. By this date there were only about six weeks to go before the whole board became irrelevant; passenger services were withdrawn from Okehampton to Bude and from Halwill to Wadebridge on 3 October 1966.
John Meredith/Online Transport Archive

A busy scene at Halwill Junction on 18 August 1966 sees examples of both the Gloucester RCW-built Class 122 and Pressed Steel-built Class 121 diesel railcars in service. On the left can be seen Nos W55014 and W55026 forming a service from Okehampton to Bude whilst on, on the right, can be seen No W55001 which has just arrived on a service from Wadebridge. No W55001 was to become departmental No DB975023 in June 1969 and has been subsequently preserved. No W55014 was also eventually to be transferred to departmental stock as No TDB975994 although its fate was different; it was scrapped by Vic Berry in October 1988. Also preserved, after being reallocated to departmental stock (as No TDB977624) in October 1992, was No W55026.
John Meredith/Online Transport Archive

The first station to be encountered on the North Devon & Cornwall Junction Railway after departing from Halwill was Hole, which is pictured from a down train on 26 May 1964. The building was typical of those on the line and included a waiting room, a goods store and a gentlemen's lavatory. The station had two platforms, each of which were 167ft in length, and two freight sidings (although freight facilities were withdrawn on 7 September 1964). Since closure the station has been converted into a private house and the grounds adapted to serve as a camp site.
Tony Wickens/Online Transport Archive

On 26 May 1964 Ivatt 2-6-2T 41214 stands in the station at Hatherleigh at 4.54pm with the 4pm service from Torrington to Halwill. Serving the town of Hatherleigh, the station was about two miles from the settlement it purported to serve and opened with the North Devon & Cornwall Junction Light Railway on 27 July 1925. Introduced in 1946, a total of 130 of George Ivatt's Class 2MT 2-6-2T design were built between then and 1952. Constructed primarily for cross-country and branch line working, a number of the type were transferred to the West Country to replace older locomotives. No 41214 was completed at Swindon Works in September 1948; transferred to Plymouth Friary in December 1961, when recorded here it was towards the end of an 18-month allocation to Barnstaple Junction. Its final reallocation – in August 1964 – saw it move to Templecombe from where it was withdrawn in July the following year.
Tony Wickens/Online Transport Archive

The first railway south from Torrington was the 3ft 0in gauge Torrington & Marland Railway, which was built to carry china clay from the quarries at Meeth to Torrington. Surveyed by John Clough, the line opened in 1880. The North Devon & Cornwall Junction Light Railway was authorised on 28 August 1914 but war delayed construction and work did not commence until 30 June 1922 with Col Holman F. Stephens as the engineer. For the first 5½ miles south from Torrington, the line made use of the erstwhile

Torrington & Marland. Although operated from opening on 17 July 1925 by the Southern, the ND&CJLR was nominally independent until Nationalisation. Petrockstow station – pictured here from the west on 19 July 1949 – served the community of Petrockstowe (sic) which was about a mile distant. The limited freight facilities at the station were withdrawn on 9 September 1964.
John Meredith/Online Transport Archive

The original line south from Torrington was the 3ft 0in gauge Torrington & Marland Railway. The mineral railway was engineered by John Barraclough Fell to provide a means of moving ball clay from various sites in north Devon to Torrington. The line, which extended eventually to 6¼ miles from Torrington to Marland, included 10 wooden built viaducts, including one across the River Torridge at Torrington. When the bulk of the mineral line was rebuilt in the early 1920s for conversion into the standard gauge North Devon & Cornwall Junction Light Railway the wooden viaducts were rebuilt. This view of Torrington Viaduct was taken looking from the north-east on 17 July 1949 and shows to good effect the then recently new single-track bridge. Although not visible in the photograph, it is still possible to see traces of the foundations for the wooden viaduct in the valley. The viaduct is still extent, now forming part of the long-distance footpath along the disused railway. *John Meredith/Online Transport Archive*

Taken from the overbridge looking north on 17 July 1949, Class E1R No 32696 is pictured having just arrived in Torrington station with a southbound service. Torrington station originally opened as the terminus from the line from Barnstaple on 18 July 1872 following the completion of the section from the previous terminus at Bideford. It was to remain a terminus station until the opening of the North Devon & Cornwall Junction Light Railway's line to Halwill on 27 July 1925. Passenger services were withdrawn to Halwill on 1 March 1965 and north to Barnstaple Junction on 4 October 1965, although there was a brief return of services from Barnstaple to Bideford in January 1968 due to flooding. Visible in front of the goods shed is a six-wheel milk wagon; milk was a significant traffic flow from Torrington and was to survive until 1978. The goods shed was demolished in the mid-1970s, and alternative means of handling the milk introduced, when a new depot to handle fertiliser traffic was constructed. This traffic was, however, not to last long – being withdrawn in January 1980 – with the line northwards to Bideford closing completely three years later.

John Meredith/Online Transport Archive

The new order at Torrington sees North British diesel-hydraulic Type 2 (later Class 22) No D6339 having arrived at Torrington from Barnstaple Junction on 26 May 1964. Following the disembarkation of any passengers, the train will be reversed to permit the connecting steam-hauled service to Halwill – visible in the background – to enter the station. The 58-strong Class 22, which was nicknamed 'Baby Warship', was introduced in 1959 with No D6339 being completed in Glasgow in April 1962. Allocated to Laira when new, the locomotive was to spend its entire operational career being based there or at Newton Abbot. The arrival of the more powerful 'Hymek' and 'Warship' classes saw the type relegated to secondary duties, including services over the ex-SR lines, but the bankruptcy of North British at the end of 1962 – which resulted in problems in obtaining spares – allied to the general reduction of traction needs as the drastic cuts following the Beeching Report took effect, meant that the type had a short operational life. No D6339 was, after being reinstated earlier in the year, one of the last quartet operational; all four were stored by the end of December 1971 and officially withdrawn on 1 January 1972. *Tony Wickens/Online Transport Archive*

Authorised on 4 August 1853, the 6½-mile broad gauge Bideford Extension Railway was designed to extend the existing North Devon Railway & Dock Co line from Fremington to Bideford. Opened on 2 November 1855, operation of the line was leased to Thomas Brassey and operated in conjunction with the North Devon. The LSWR took over the lease on 1 August 1862 and formally absorbed the line on 1 January 1865. The station illustrated here was the result of relocation following the opening of the standard gauge line to Torrington on 18 July 1872. Formal powers to remove the broad gauge track over the line to Fremington was obtained on 13 July 1876. Ivatt No 41216, seen here at the head of a southbound service towards Halwill, was completed at Crewe Works in 1948; based on the Western Region from September 1961, it was transferred to Barnstaple Junction in February 1963 and to Exmouth Junction in November 1964. A final move, in June 1965, saw it reallocated to Templecombe, from where it was withdrawn in March 1966. There remains a railway presence at Bideford as it is home to the Bideford Railway Heritage Centre.
Martin Jenkins/Online Transport Archive

Viewed looking north towards the buffer stocks at Ilfracombe on 27 May 1964, a DMU stands in the distance at the platform awaiting departure. Although there had been earlier proposals to provide a railway connection to the town, it was the LSWR-backed Barnstaple & Ilfracombe Railway – authorised on 4 July 1870 – that was to prove successful. The heavily-engineered and steeply-graded 15-mile line from Barnstaple Junction was eventually opened on 20 July 1874. Following complete closure on 5 October 1970 and the abortive attempt at the line's preservation, the station was demolished after 1972 and a factory was built on the site.
Tony Wickens/Online Transport Archive

On 12 September 1965 the Southern Counties Touring Society organised the 'Exeter Flyer' rail tour from Waterloo to Ilfracombe and Torrington. The whole train ran through to Barnstaple Junction where it was divided. One section, headed by Standard 2-6-4T No 80043 headed to the latter whilst another of the class – No 80039 – hauled the section to Ilfracombe and back. Pictured running round its train at Ilfracombe in the early afternoon – its booked departure time was 2.55pm – is No 80039 which was, at the time, allocated to Templecombe. No 80039 was withdrawn in January the following year. This view, taken looking towards the south, shows to good effect the small single-track concrete-built engine shed that was opened by the Southern Railway in 1928. The facilities included a 65ft turntable and a coal stage; however, the shed was closed by BR during 1964.
John Meredith/Online Transport Archive

Unrebuilt 'Battle of Britain' No 34081 *92 Squadron* approaches Mortehoe & Woolacombe station from the north as it passes under the B3343 road bridge with an up service from Ilfracombe to Salisbury in September 1959. No 34081 was completed at Brighton Works in September. Allocated to Ramsgate for Kent Coast services, the locomotive was transferred to Exmouth Junction in October 1957. In June 1964, the locomotive was transferred again – this time to Eastleigh – before withdrawal two months later. In April 1965 No 34081 was moved to Woodham Bros at Barry for scrap in the company of Nos 34057 and 34067. Eight years later No 34081 was purchased for preservation by the Battle of Britain Locomotive Preservation Society; after a quarter of a century of work, No 34081 re-entered service on the Nene Valley Railway in 1998. It is still based on that line. *Derek Cross*

In September 1959 unrebuilt 'Battle of Britain' No 34079 *141 Squadron* is seen at Braunton with a down service from London Waterloo to Ilfracombe. Completed at Brighton in July 1948, No 34079 had initially been allocated to Ramsgate when new. Transferred to Stewarts Lane in 1954, the Pacific was one of the class rendered surplus to requirements in south-east England as a result of electrification and was transferred to Exmouth Junction in February 1958. A final transfer – in September 1964 – saw No 34079 move to Eastleigh, from where it was withdrawn in February 1966. *Derek Cross*

On 18 July 1949 a Class M7 0-4-4T – No 44 (still in Southern condition despite Nationalisation being more than 18 months earlier) – is seen crossing the viaduct over the River Taw between Barnstaple Town and Barnstaple Junction with an up freight service. At this date the locomotive was allocated to Barnstaple Junction shed; it was destined to remain there until mid-May 1951 when it was reallocated to Exmouth Junction from where it was withdrawn in September 1961. The single-track viaduct was completed for the opening of the line to Ilfracombe on 20 July 1874. The original Barnstaple Town station – known as Barnstaple Quay when first opened – was replaced by a new station, slightly closer to Ilfracombe, on 16 May 1898 when it became the western terminus of the 1ft 11½in Lynton & Barnstaple line. The line from Barnstaple Junction to Ilfracombe closed completely following the last train on 3 October 1970; although there were efforts made to preserve the route, these came to nothing – the North Devon Railway Co being unable to raise the £500,000 needed to reopen the line – and the track was lifted in late 1974. The viaduct across the Taw was demolished in 1978.
John Meredith/Online Transport Archive

A second view of the River Taw viaduct in Barnstaple sees 'West Country' No 34025 *Whimple* at the head of the up 'Devon Belle' as it approaches Barnstaple Junction. New in March 1946, the locomotive briefly carried the named *Rough Tor* in 1948 before being renamed *Whimple* in May of the same year. Allocated to Exmouth Junction when recorded here, No 34025 was reallocated to Bricklayers Arms in October 1957 – after having been rebuilt – and was finally withdrawn from Bournemouth shed in July 1967 following the end of main-line steam operation out of London Waterloo. The Pullman 'Devon Belle' service was launched by the Southern Railway on 20 June 1947 and featured an observation coach at the rear for passengers to enjoy the views of the line to Ilfracombe; the train initially operated with two sections – from Ilfracombe and Plymouth – but the Plymouth portion was dropped in September 1949. The surviving Waterloo-Ilfracombe 'Devon Belle' service was withdrawn at the end of the summer season in 1954.
D. Kelk/Online Transport Archive

On 18 July 1949, Class N 2-6-0 No 31409 approaches Barnstaple Junction, having just crossed the River Taw with a two-coach train formed of ex-GWR coaching stock. An additional 15 Class Ns were constructed by the Southern between 1932 and 1934 at Ashford Works; these were equipped with larger – 4,000 gallon – tenders. No 1409 was completed in October 1933 and was to be physically renumbered 31409 in January 1949. Based at Exmouth Junction at Nationalisation, the locomotive was transferred to Ashford almost exactly a decade after this photograph was taken. However, its return to Kent was destined to be relatively short-lived as it was reallocated back to Exmouth Junction in November 1961. It lasted a further 12 months in service before withdrawal in November 1962; it was one of the first two of the batch built in the 1930s to be withdrawn.
John Meredith/Online Transport Archive

Taken looking in the down direction from the station footbridge on 26 May 1964, this view records the junction between the lines heading north to Ilfracombe and west towards Bideford. Barnstaple Junction was rebuilt in the early 1870s to cater for the opening of the line to Ilfracombe on 20 July 1874. Following the closure of the Ilfracombe line on 5 October 1970, the station reverted to its pre-1874 name of simply Barnstaple. Freight traffic continued west of Barnstaple as far as Meeth until china clay traffic ceased in March 1983. Visible in the background is Barnstaple Junction West signalbox. *Tony Wickens/Online Transport Archive*

A hint of the line's future on 19 July 1949 as ex-GWR 2-6-2T No 5522 passes through the junction to the west of Barnstaple Junction light engine. Completed at Swindon Works in December 1927, No 5522 was one of the '4575' class designed by Charles Collett and first introduced in February 1927. A total of 100 of the type were constructed between then and February 1929. Although No 5522 was withdrawn in March 1959 from Taunton shed and scrapped the next month, sister locomotive No 5521 is one of 11 of the class to survive in preservation.
John Meredith/Online Transport Archive

On 18 July 1949 Drummond-designed Class M7 No 247 – still bearing its Southern Railway number and livery – is pictured shunting coaching stock at Barnstaple Junction station. The track heading off to the left – the north – is the line towards Barnstaple Town and Ilfracombe. A total of 104 of this class of 0-4-4T were constructed for the LSWR between 1897 and 1911, with No 247 (BR No 30247) being completed at Nine Elms in April 1897. All 104 passed to BR ownership at Nationalisation and all bar one – No 672 (withdrawn without being renumbered during 1948) – were still in service at the end of 1956; withdrawals then saw the numbers reduced so that only 14 were still operational at the end of 1963 and all had succumbed by the end of the following year. No 247 was allocated to Barnstaple Junction when recorded here; it was based at Nine Elms for two months at the end of 1952 before returning to Barnstaple Junction, from where it was withdrawn in October 1961.

John Meredith/Online Transport Archive

With the now roofless engine shed in the background – it was closed four months later – unrebuilt 'West Country' No 34020 *Seaton* stands in the platform at Barnstaple Junction at 3.10pm with the down 'Atlantic Coast Express' to Ilfracombe on 26 May 1964. Completed in December 1945 and formally named the following June, No 34020 had been transferred from Nine Elms to Exmouth Junction in late May 1962. Two years later the locomotive was approaching the end of its career; it was withdrawn four months later.
Tony Wickens/Online Transport Archive

With the small engine shed in the background, unrebuilt 'Battle of Britain' No 34072 *257 Squadron* is pictured awaiting departure from Barnstaple Junction with an up service on 3 June 1961. New in April 1948 and initially allocated to Dover, No 34072 was based at Exmouth Junction between February 1958 and June 1964, when it was transferred to Eastleigh from where it was withdrawn four months later. Sold to Woodham Bros, the remains of the locomotive were sold for preservation in 1984. Its restoration was completed in 1990. The original shed at Barnstaple Junction was located to the east of the station but was replaced in 1863 by the two-road wooden-built structure illustrated here. Originally slated, the roof was replaced by corrugated iron – as shown here – towards the end of Southern Railway era. The condition of the shed deteriorated prior to its final closure in September 1964; it was demolished shortly thereafter.
J. Joyce/Online Transport Archive

On 6 June 1964 the crew of unrebuilt 'Battle of Britain' No 34083 *605 Squadron* pick up the token at Umberleigh as it heads an up service towards Exeter. Umberleigh, which originally opened courtesy of the North Devon Railway on 1 August 1854, remains operational although the station is now reduced to a single platform with station building on the down side. This must have been amongst the last duties undertake by the locomotive; it was withdrawn from Exmouth Junction shed early the next month and scrapped during June 1965.
John Meredith/Online Transport Archive

During September 1959, '700' class 0-6-0 No 30691 approaches Copplestone with the up pick-up freight from Barnstaple to Exeter. Prior to becoming Locomotive Engineer (Chief Mechanical Engineer from 1895) with the LSWR in 1895, Dugald Drummond had held similar roles with both the North British and Caledonian railways. For both he had designed 0-6-0 freight locomotives and the 30-strong '700' class, introduced in 1897, was very similar to those produced for the latter. All were built in Glasgow by Dübs & Co and were known latterly as 'Black Motors'. Between 1921 and 1929 all were modified to the design of Robert Urie; this involved lengthening the frames to accommodate an extended smokebox, being fitted with superheaters and increased cylinder diameter. New in March 1897, No 30691 had been allocated to Salisbury before a final transfer, in December 1954, saw it move to Exmouth Junction. It was withdrawn in July 1961 and scrapped two months later.
Derek Cross

In July 1951 'West Country' No 34030 *Watersmeet* heads towards the Coleford Junction to the north of Yeoford with a service from London to Plymouth. Yeoford station was opened by the North Devon Railway on 1 August 1854. The line towards Okehampton, authorised on 17 July 1862, was opened from Coleford Junction to North Tawton on 1 November 1865. The Okehampton Railway became the Devon & Cornwall Railway on 26 July 1870; backed by the LSWR, the Devon & Cornwall was formally acquired by the LSWR on 1 January 1872. No 34030 emerged from Brighton Works in May 1946; allocated to Exmouth Junction in October 1948, it was to spend the rest of its operational life based there before withdrawal in September 1964. *Derek Cross*

A decade later – on 27 May 1964 – modern traction has replaced steam as a three-car DMU stands in the platform at Yeoford at 5.31pm with the 5.5pm service from Exeter Central to Ilfracombe. *Tony Wickens/Online Transport Archive*

Although the LSWR had plans to construct its own station between Exeter Central and the line towards Coleford Junction, these were never completed and, as a result, Southern services to and from the Withered Arm used the GWR's St David's station. In August 1959 unrebuilt 'West Country' No 34108 *Wincanton* stands in St David's station with an up service. One of the class to be completed after Nationalisation, No 34108 emerged from Brighton Works in April 1950 and was initially allocated to Bournemouth. Transferred to Exmouth Junction in February 1958, it was to be rebuilt in May 1961. A final transfer, in November 1963, saw it move to Salisbury, from where it was withdrawn in June 1967 during the final run-down of Southern Region steam. *LRTA (London Area) Collection/Online Transport Archive*